P9-DGB-630

PENGUIN BOOKS

MIXOLOGY

ADRIAN MATEJKA is a graduate of the Southern Illinois University Carbondale MFA program. The author of *The Devil's Garden*, his work has appeared in the *American Poetry Review*, *Gulf Coast*, *Crab Orchard Review*, and *Prairie Schooner*. He teaches creative writing and English literature at Southern Illinois University Edwardsville.

THE NATIONAL POETRY SERIES

The National Poetry Series was established in 1978 to ensure the publication of five poetry books annually through five participating publishers. Publication is funded by the Lannan Foundation; Stephen Graham; Joyce & Seward Johnson Foundation; Glenn and Renee Schaeffer, Juliet Lea Hillman Simonds Foundation; and, Charles B. Wright III.

2008 COMPETITION WINNERS

Anna Journey of Houston, Texas,
  If Birds Gather Your Hair for Nesting
Chosen by Thomas Lux, to be published by University of Georgia Press

Douglas Kearney of Van Nuys, California,
  The Black Automaton
Chosen by Catherine Wagner, to be published by Fence Books

Adrian Matejka of Edwardsville, Illinois,
  Mixology
Chosen by Kevin Young, to be published by Penguin Books

Kristin Naca of Minneapolis, Minnesota,
  Bird Eating Bird
Chosen by Yusef Komunyakaa for The National Poetry Series mtvU Prize, to be published by HarperCollins Publishers

Sarah O'Brien of Brookfield, Ohio,
  catch light
Chosen by David Shapiro, to be published by Coffee House Press

MIXology

ADRIAN MATEJKA

 PENGUIN BOOKS

PENGUIN BOOKS
Published by the Penguin Group
Penguin Group (USA) Inc., 375 Hudson Street, New York, New York 10014, U.S.A.
Penguin Group (Canada), 90 Eglinton Avenue East, Suite 700, Toronto, Ontario,
Canada M4P 2Y3 (a division of Pearson Penguin Canada Inc.) · Penguin Books
Ltd, 80 Strand, London WC2R 0RL, England · Penguin Ireland, 25 St Stephen's
Green, Dublin 2, Ireland (a division of Penguin Books Ltd) · Penguin Group
(Australia), 250 Camberwell Road, Camberwell, Victoria 3124, Australia (a
division of Pearson Australia Group Pty Ltd) · Penguin Books India Pvt Ltd,
11 Community Centre, Panchsheel Park, New Delhi – 110 017, India · Penguin
Group (NZ), 67 Apollo Drive, Rosedale, North Shore 0632, New Zealand (a
division of Pearson New Zealand Ltd) · Penguin Books (South Africa) (Pty)
Ltd, 24 Sturdee Avenue, Rosebank, Johannesburg 2196, South Africa

Penguin Books Ltd, Registered Offices:
80 Strand, London WC2R 0RL, England

First published in Penguin Books 2009

10 9 8 7 6 5 4 3 2 1

Copyright © Adrian Matejka, 2009
All rights reserved

Pages ix–x constitute an extension of this copyright page.

LIBRARY OF CONGRESS CATALOGING IN PUBLICATION DATA
Matejka, Adrian.
    Mixology / Adrian Matejka.
    p. cm.
    ISBN 978-0-14-311583-0
    1. Race—Poetry. I. Title.
    PS3613.A825M59 2009
    811'.6—dc22
                                    2009005805

Printed in the United States of America
Set in Fournier MT with Landry Gothic · Designed by Sabrina Bowers

Except in the United States of America, this book is sold subject to the condition
that it shall not, by way of trade or otherwise, be lent, resold, hired out, or other-
wise circulated without the publisher's prior consent in any form of binding or
cover other than that in which it is published and without a similar condition
including this condition being imposed on the subsequent purchaser.

The scanning, uploading and distribution of this book via the Internet or via any
other means without the permission of the publisher is illegal and punishable by
law. Please purchase only authorized electronic editions, and do not participate in
or encourage electronic piracy of copyrighted materials. Your support of the
author's rights is appreciated.

FOR MARLEY AND STACEY

ACKNOWLEDGMENTS

Thank you to the editors of the journals in which these poems have appeared:

Salt Hill Journal: "Do the Right Thing," "This Be The Verse"

Crab Orchard Review: "Language Mixology," "Synth Composite Basketball: No more Leather," "Tyndall Armory"

Drunken Boat: "Beneath the Bass Line," " 'Samson and Delilah' "

Gulf Coast: "Maggot Brain," "Tommy Johnson"

Indiana Review: "Affirmative Action"

LIT: "Bob Kaufman Trip"

Mot Juste: "What the Dead are Missing Out On:"

Natural Bridge: " 'America's First and Foremost Black Superstar,' " "Colloquialisms"

Ninth Letter: "Babel by Foot"

Painted Bride Quarterly: "Domo Arigato, Mr. Mulatto (Dub Style)," "Ode to Fela (1938–97)," " 'Where o Where is the Blues?' Blues,"

Pleiades: "Mulatto Ego Remix," "Synth Composite Basketball: No More Fundamentals"

Prairie Schooner: "Sampled Biography," "Seven Days of Falling," "Wheels of Steel," "Winter / Weird Fishes"

"Landscaped Postcard as Jimi Hendrix" appears in the anthology *Kiss the Sky: Fiction and Poetry Starring Jimi Hendrix* (Paycock Press, 2007)

"Affirmative Action" was selected for Metro Arts in Transit and the Poetry Society of America 2008 Poetry in Motion Series

"Language Mixology" also appeared on Verse Daily (www.versedaily.org) (May 10, 2006)

Some of the poems also appear in text and audio form at From the Fishouse (www.fishousepoems.org).

Thank you to the gang of artists whose generosity helped shape these poems in one way or another: Willis Barnstone, Stacey Lynn Brown, Cornelius Eady, Paul Guest, Major Jackson, Rodney Jones, A. Van Jordan, Melanie Jordan, Allison Joseph, Douglas Kearney, Ruth Ellen Kocher, Yusef Komunyakaa, Quraysh Ali Lansana, Shara McCallum, Kevin Neireiter, Marilyn Nelson, April Ossmann, Greg Pardlo, Oliver de la Paz, Hilda Raz, Cedric Ross, Matthew Shenoda, Sean Singer, Jon Tribble, Frank X. Walker, Daniel Wideman, the *River Styx* basketball posse, my SIUE clique, and to my family, real and imagined.

Many thanks also to the National Poetry Series, Paul Slovak at Penguin, and Kevin Young for selecting the book.

CONTENTS

WHEELS OF STEEL

MiXology

SEVEN DAYS OF FALLING

Today, I'm assimilating like margarine
into hotcakes. I'm getting down

like Danny LaRusso after the against-
the-rules leg sweep. So low,

I'll be a flower in common decency's
lapel. Factual, the same way "Zanzibar"

means *sea of blacks* to anyone who isn't
from there. Where is Juan Valdez,

his burroesque dependability when
you need him? I had a friend who minted

t-shirts with Juan front and center,
an afro instead of a sombrero, a power

fist in place of a smile. The inscription:
100% Colombian. I'm going the way

of skin—radio waves, thoughts
like ear-to-ear transmissions grounded

into the ozone on the way from mindless
space to forgetful Earth. Man, my skin

doesn't need me any more than mold
needs cheese. On this day of cellophane

lunchboxes and hand grenades reshaping
my palms into their own militaristic orbit,

there are only oceans to catch me.
On this day, something needs

to catalogue me: a hall monitor
doubled wide by ambition,

a goldfish with thumbs hitchhiking
toward a fishbowl full of dub.

DOMO ARIGATO, MR. MULATTO (DUB STYLE)

SAMPLE ONE:

You're wondering who I am /
am-am-a-ah-we-ammmmm . . .

I have a mish-mash falsetto:
vigorous, robotic like a biter nibbling
some other emcee for a rumor
of validity. Kids call it *hateration*,

but in this here world of Dictaphones
and stethoscopes, one brown
is as bad as the next. It doesn't
matter if the pigment is seasonal

or gene pooled in a euphoria
of sun spots. It's the falsetto, not
the tongue clicking *dis* but meaning
dat in the mix. It's the falsetto—

a better idea than explanation
like an umbrella made of handkerchiefs.
Better in person than polaroids
like a sponge bath of fingerprints.

SAMPLE TWO:

I've got a see-see-secret I've
b-e-E-eeeeen hiding
under my sk-sk-skiwee-wee-in . . .

Fingerprints in my sponge bath,
a squabble between appearance
and what is meant like Denzel

telling Ethan, *Muthafucka, anger
is waking up with a bad goatee.*
At least that's what he should

have said. I used to get mad
that Denzel won his Oscar for playing
a roped-out G until I realized

playing and *being* are both gerunds.
There is a password for understanding
skin, but it's more lack of observation

on your end, homie. When the sun
shines, it's blinging outside. Even if
your shades are drawn, homie.

SAMPLE THREE:

*I am . . . I iƺam . . .
the modern ma-ma-ma-hn,
who hides behind a ma-weeee-ask . . .*

Homie, don't blame the Halloween
masks, scuba masks, eye

and mouth joints used to rob
the corner market for your lack

of bling. My mask has teeth
and tear marks like bison meat.

Open sockets like somebody
took the bulbs out. It fits

easily in a sack of nomenclature
without clout. And all the ladies

saying, *Yeah, Yeah, Yeah* . . .
There once was a white boy

who could get into all the parties
using the same story:

*My mother used to sing backup
for Funkadelic.* Until some

hating somebody asked if he
really understood what that meant.

SAMPLE FOUR:

*Thank . . . Thank . . . Thank . . .
YOU ve-er-ery much / much / much . . .
muwi-much . . . Mr. Mulatto*

Understand the meaning of *dis*
and *dat*, the etymology
of shark-fin hats and bullet scraps.
We know some things, man,

about some things: genealogy
squib-kicked between pigment's
rusted railings. Cardboard
shaped as windows, reminders
that any day is a good day.
Suns go up and down,
but in the diesel lean
of cracked-out brick for buildings,
brown folks go from here
to whatever's after in a shufflebuck
of goatees. Time is the on
and off of street lamps. Never mind
prayer hands shaped like leaves
falling back into the lap because
they're tired of waiting. Never
mind the lake tide taking a breather
from the constancy of pulling.
All that dragging around brings
nothing but milk cartons
and habitually sideways fish
staring at our geography
with slot tokens instead of eyes.
And for Mr. Mulatto, the sun
blings yet another perfect day.

AFFIRMATIVE ACTION

I'm caught in a bouquet of skin
and hair. Slaves, up and down
my blood like a boot in mud.
A constellation of *almost haves*

and *never knews* pointing north.
That's why my childhood is a handful
of oceans and warped wood, shaken
like dice. Hopscotch lips, double ply

knees. On the one hand, sand and spit.
On the other, a coffle of spiders
eating under a split fist moon.
Free means artifice. Being free

means standing on a stanchion
of jive, black face or otherwise.

"WHERE O WHERE IS THE BLUES?" BLUES

I just found me some blues glued
and jimmied into a milk bottle's neck.

Four foot leeward from flipping the script.
Four latitude and four long

from the back-step on the extra beat.
Wind and dirt, salt and gut-strings—

mimicking the straight talk the sailor talks,
crooked in his seat. Teeth or no,

somebody's got to do the talking.
Even if the Dirty South compass

is store-bought and made to scratch a beat.
A needle is used to scratching

like women are used to fighting,
but nails aren't supposed to be more

than cherry-blossom shingling.
In this world of momentous occasions

I'm all wine cap underneath.
So rubber stamp your sterno ticket

with glee like Jazzy Jeff
hand-clasping a part on the Will

Smith show. Jeff's a real G—
reminder for reminder's sake.

How else is there to avoid being left
behind once syndication hits?

And Jazzy was the one with chops.
The bottle works the ocean like blues

get worked by a pine guitar kit.
The same way a mannequin

would make all kinds of music
about being a man if it could.

SYNTH COMPOSITE BASKETBALL:
NO MORE FUNDAMENTALS

Check out Iverson and his jim-braid retroactivism—
cross handles over because a hand can forget
how to stay sober. A hand can forget how to handle

like microwaves don't remember how to pop
the corn, how to warm the beef. Now that's a neck
to neck schism, even without the gold teeth.

They call it a crossover, but I like tats and funk.
I like overpriced throwbacks since before crunk.
Mall-icized, not for ball. In Champs, they

only play hip hop now and everyone is going pro.
These boys be Newton confused: going up
with no return trip. Up toward the half-moon

backboard. Up past the full moon backdap until
the ball is post-dated by some intergalactic
bitch slap: *Not in my house,* says the middle-ager

at the Y. These boys be one less chapter to read
in science books. These hops be invalidating
gravity's flow and push. These non-pollsters,

sitting on dubs, riding circles. Like that bus full
of criminals in the Method Man video.
White boys sampling *And One* videos.

Can I not get a run? Where is the lift, the rotation
of the ball moving like hand-polished rims
that keep their spun even when the car stops?

TYNDALL ARMORY

Public Enemy had no idea of what
to do on a stage in 1987, but we
didn't know what to do as rap crowd either.
Attendance was mandatory, jammed
into the Tyndall Armory, one night
after amateur boxing and one night
before bingo. A bunch of homeboys
kenti-ed together with African medallions,
graffiti spray-painted jeans—all of us
mad at the conspiracy of conspiracy,
staring each other down with a circular
anger only black men can justify.
Terminator X—his one-handed power
fist cut and scratch already perfected—
was the only thing keeping the crowd
from getting started. Bass lines, warning
sirens transformed into samples refusing
The Wop like the black maître
at the Highlands Country Club refused
to seat black people. My friend Richard
was determined to be the first black
president, refused wine coolers and weed,
white women and white lines because
the man could hold anything against him
during a campaign. As president,
he would buy Highlands and turn it into
a black thing. Terminator X had Rich
ready to say *peace* to the presidency
and Nat Turner the first patch of white
he saw. And when Chuck D mugged
the stage, African medallion swinging

like left hooks, baseball cap pulled down
so low his eyes were the idea of eyes,
the heat in that room was enough to make
any Tom reconsider his friendships.

DO THE RIGHT THING

Spike Lee is so small I didn't even
see him at first, surrounded

by Black Expo goers like a gumdrop
in a fist. When I asked him to sign

my "Free South Africa" t-shirt,
he said, *You didn't buy that at this*

booth. Fresh off seeing *Do the Right
Thing*, I crowed: "What's that got

to do with your movies?" His fans
laughed, so he edited me like my name

was Pino: *Why you care? You
ain't even black.* Someone behind

me said, *Damn, Spike. That ain't
right.* But Spike's shamed scribble

on my t-shirt didn't change the missed
free throw feeling in my chest.

SYNTH COMPOSITE BASKETBALL: NO MORE LEATHER

This sorry ball: mulatto
of homemade leather and rubber
now named a "basketball"

hyperventilates from concrete
to palm like a little kid,
bitched out on time out.

The bounce bounces according
to pressure and rotation,
but this isn't basketball.

Even with punks jumping
high enough to shotty physics.
Even with Jams revisited

as athletic shorts. My basketball
has defensive stance, two hands
on the rock. Jumper elbows

at angles like nose caricatures
on the Boardwalk. Socks up
and short shorts. Rust makes

my hands hurt, busts jumpers
and lungs. All my theories
and historic stamina left

in the Gus Macker me and my team
almost won. *No "I" in team*
phonetics left on the outside courts

at Ben Davis High School,
where dudes talking that *When
I balled in school* got Statue

of Libertied by Terence Stansbury
or shook by Vern Fleming's
behind-the-back dribble. That's

basketball, as pure as Dr. J saving
Pittsburgh. Or the actor formerly
known as Jimmy Chitwood hitting

the game-winner, even though
he got cut from Cathedral's varsity
before Hollywood. He couldn't

make the same team we beat
like Rock'em Sock'em.
That was before I was rubbing

a half-moon gut under a half-moon
backboard in the elementary school
parking lot. Back before touching

one toe, then the other needed a map.
Basketball works like carbon dating
on spine and handles. Not love handles—

hands trying to work the dribble
with something missing. The same
way a bad comic works the funny.

WINTER / WEIRD FISHES

—*after Radiohead*

Every morning, you loiter
like a middle-aged sugar mama
once the sun's up, hoping
to be more than a meal ticket.
You are a skeleton, wishing
for the plaster attention
of being broken. Winter,
this is your intervention.
The kind of stop-gap
where the breakers break,
their short sleeves tightly
remind of the kindness
in summer's skezzey whirlwinds.
The kind of meeting
where everyone is a drunk
uncle at a magic show.
The moment the handkerchief
becomes a fist of flowers:
Them flowers came out
your sleeve, boy! I miss Seattle
where your arthritic flakes
are treated like the Serengeti
if it were a break-up song
on skip. Since I can't make
it back west on a budget,
I'm going down south—
home of hanging trees, nooses
knotted as accessories. America's
sandwichless crust: Houston.
To the bottom, to escape,
where every cloudless day
works like homemade novocaine.

BABEL BY FOOT

Black folks in Eugene are coffee
shop ideas like *carbuncle*
or *mulatto, coffles,* or *integration,*

but I have never seen so many
mixed children rocking skin's
simplicity in one place. Always,

white moms toting brown babies
in the grocery by themselves.
K-solo we used to call it. Always,

the task of definition falling
on those with consideration enough,
guilt enough to leave open the option

of passing. An understanding of skin,
of pigment's capacity like the original
enabler, Thomas Jefferson.

Eyesight flickering, a return
to the big plantation in the sky nigh
at hand and he turned to math

to salvage his offspring. With quill
and ink, he figured three generations
of stirring white into black makes

white enough. Even though
it doesn't work whistling the theme
from *Shaft*. Even though it doesn't

work with house paint, rumors
about rumors, paper-ballot voting,
or the soft belly of musical notes.

Call it paternal instinct—color *isn't,*
rather than *is* like Chet Baker trying
his Sunday best to be Miles.

White chicks other than Janis
trying on the blues like a marked down
dress. All of us, half-breeding legality

since 1967. Half-casting in the eye
of a spinning rim. The most
ergonomic people in the world

fanning different faces like a card
shark's never-losing cards on our way
back to Babel. One good foot

at a time, James Brown said.
Man, we work color the same
way curb feelers work necessity.

Graveyard
Attire

BOB KAUFMAN TRIP

For Bob Kaufman (1925–1986)

In the unravel of circumstance
and clout, some things
remain hinged: the manifesto

of three-eyed sight
and funk-sight, piss smelling
of jail cells. Jails hemmed

from lowest-bid concrete
and tin cups manhandled
in a ribcage.

In a universe of falsettos—
who ain't a troubadour?
The lock pick.

In a world made from water—
who ain't aquatic?
The lock, baby.

A buzzard perches on
the crucifix of my head.
Bob, mad-lib me a fresco

of brick and bar. Haiku
the story the story tells
quickly, like Q-Tip

and his El Segundo party.
Give me cranial, discarded
on diner napkins, scribbled

Mad Dog bags, lifetimes
forgotten every so often
like fishes forget.

1986: wandering San Fran
wild-eyed and wheezing trochees,
even if people in France

still remembered you.
What profit is in blood
when down in the pit?

Nathan: no room for the riff
of tambourines in wine-light.
No *fromage*: no room for you.

"PETE'S BLUES"

For Roy Buchanan (1939–1988)

Roy Buchanan sent
The Rolling Stones
packing. He said,
I'm straight to leather
retrospectives, to A-G-
D progressions. *Peace
out* from the same
Buchanan who enrolled
in barber school
because no label wanted
him full time.
The booze and lemon
pledge Buchanan
who choked lyrics,
called it *singing* since
guitar strings and vocal
cords are made
from different kinds
of wheat. In a cell
again, he wished
for watermelon, a place
to spit. He wished
for a woman other
than the one
that got him locked
up with blackberry
seeds instead of lips.
Tap water in a glass.
Something striated
like a rainbow
to make lights-out
organic. Forget

the psychedelic records
he cut to make rent:
real music came
from those liquor-
taxed fingers. See
it in the ladies,
singing like it's
the last song
after the very last
song as he cat claws
through the six of them.
Or see him string
with a switchblade
instead of a slide.
See him hung
by his own hand
during that two-bit bid.

MAGGOT BRAIN

For Eddie Hazel (1950–1992)

Jawbone used for a washboard.
Scrape of knuckles, whelped

skin from washing bumps,
from washing needles or mosquitoes.

Or fishscale rails, maggot brain.
Teeth, stickling a long dream—

click of brain, click of mousetrap
on the four-fingered way down.

Click: that's what happens
when George Clinton says

said *Play like yo' mama just died*.
Everything else becomes a handful

of stomach aches, maggot brain.
The cavity of a jail cell smells

like everything a man wants gone.
Not *funky*, but nasty. Not nasty,

because nobody's trying to shank
you in the shower. Just a big

time out with bologna sandwiches
and bad fruit. Jail is a mouthful

of twitches and aches, maggot brain.
Ain't you supposed to rise to the top

of this mess like some triplicated heart?
Ain't that extra chamber below

the frets in charge of breathing?
I hear that thing wheezing

like a breath still trying to breathe.
Maggot brain, somebody

someplace is losing a mama right now:
Go maggot brain. Go maggot brain.

WHAT THE DEAD ARE MISSING OUT ON:

—*after Francisco Hernández*

Sections of a woman's body,
misappropriated angelically—
this hand, this wrist. The motion
of hand to hip, hip back to mouth.

Fresh understanding in water's
cusp. The slice of skin between
shirt and skirt appearing
and re-appearing easily in the habit

of skin. A plate of barbeque
as spicy as a girl with a reputation.
Stevie Wonder chorusing with himself
because no one else can.

Permanence, like the stains on a motel
pillow.
            Her voice, whoever she was.

"SAMSON AND DELILAH"

For Reverend Gary Davis (1896–1972)

Blind or saved, the end is the same:
guitar pick circling reverb's foxhole
like the fingers attached
to the hand attached to the person
picking uneven bills from the collection
plate in the humidity of all things
sanctified and hungry.

AN OLD HAND

For Lorenzo Thomas (1944–2005)

When we met, he was old
enough to be put together
with leaded gas and gut strings.

But this man shook my hand
like he was the lucky one.
Instead of that lucky being me,

counting up my nickels
at the end of the day, hoping
they make some kind of sense.

O you don't know the pain,
he said about a picture
of a Salvadoran girl.

This man, who wrote shouting
poems, rhyming poems,
poems winking like Redd

Foxx records. The night
we met, he read "An Old Hand"
smiling the whole time,

answer showing up before
the question: *O you don't
know the pain.* And later

that night, drunk and arguing
with my woman again, trying
to brawl a way out of Houston's

humidity like a cat in a bathtub,
I thought of that frail man.
The water of his words torn

piece by piece by cancer.
I thought of his generosity
and fought all the harder.

ODE TO FELA (1938-1997)

I. WATER NO GET ENEMY

Fela: symmetry of horn and fist.
    Oxford graduate.
        American cultural student.

Water No Get Enemy.
    Three-dimensional spliff.
        Hunger's obstinacy.

Postcolonial malaise.
    Afrobeat at the end of Lagos.
        Them talk of black power.

Poly-mass weddings.
    Water No Get Enemy.
        Black president self-styled.

One trip to jail per coup.
    Annotation of inertia.
        No music in jail.

Water No Get Enemy.
    Nigerian cabbie's day: Fela in Seattle.
        Three-spliff dimension.

Enemy, jail won't stop the naming.
    Music, funky enough to break jail.
        Military-made orphan.

I'm finished, Mother.

2. FELA'S GUITAR PLAYER ACKNOWLEDGES
THE ALPHA MALE

You say Fela is Bacchus with pigment.
English schooling gives that language.

You say he's cocksure because there
isn't another word for a man with sixty

women who still hang around to catch
that one nuptial every two months.

Alpha male, alpha male.
He's not that tall. He's not that tough.

So you check the Oxford and there's still
no word for the Black President's blue

jumpsuit strut: gap-tooth smile, that brown
highlight of politic on skin. If there

is no name for that, what's the name
for your boss playing the second set

shirtless? Bird-chest preen, cat-call singing
while some of the Queens you wish loved

you dance masculinity's circle. Alpha male,
alpha male. What's the name for you

trying to keep time with twenty-eight other
musicians? A butterfly on the down beat?

A mumble down the stairs?
Time must have reset its clock:

you missed a riff and Fela cut a look.
Even then, you were shining in sax

and trumpet like soldiers
rising up from behind the countryside.

3. WOMEN

This is why men fight: women
with that shell and bead game,

white face paint—a map away
from those hips, moving like gravity

is a parlor trick. Only the pinion
matters then. Thirty wives and thirty

mistresses, even if it was politics.
Chorus of big ones and little ones

singing quarrelsome harmonics:
You don't please Fela, you lose

your day. Over and over until
a hub cap, a handful of dirt seem right

for warring. Polyphonics spiraling
the Republic of Kalakuta

like a song that's forgotten except
the chorus: *Women with half-peeled*

moon. Women with inertia's grace
unhooking brain and bloom.

4. FELA DREAMS OF UNKNOWN SOLDIERS

You dream hectic
polysyllabics,
consolation—
an open
power fist,
put to skin—
unmindful
war chants,
cowrie shells
in dozens.
You dream
of coral snake:
lips to horn
like another
new woman.
To the left,
a refrain
of Queens
not thinking
about *obiri's*
crowd. Right,
horn stacks
shelling number

one son
Femi. Dream
of making better:
drums stretched
to feed
fire and palm.
Call to arms
when you found
mother in driveway
doubled over.
Mr. President,
you are arming:
I condemn
democracy now.

BENEATH THE BASS LINE

For Charles Mingus (1922–1979)

If claiming you retired 23 Mexican
whores in one night wasn't enough,

you used a conk to profile as south
of the border, to be even more

in touch with the culture.
Now, you're a handful of tap-dance

on the Ganges. Since mythology
is something ash likes to forget,

you are also part of the mulatto
revolution. For all those about to pass,

we salute you. Even if you played
the pimp and lied to your shrink,

thanks. Even if you watered up
like a baby because the Man asked

you to play "The Stars and Stripes
Forever." Thank you for chords

so magnanimous, they step all up
and down like an asthmatic hoodoo.

Lip Syncing
in Texas

THE ATTIC

There's no god to be found up in here.
Only gangly insects mid-migration,
using my place as a rest stop on the way
out of Texas. Wood panel hinged

to patchwork carpet like Cameros
to sideburns. Hell-bent spiders on the creep:
the softest shoe of eight-legged double-talk.
Loose-limbed beetles, bo-jangling

moths masked as dust fronds on brown
walls. These dead bugs marionette
in the webs' captivity, belly-doubling
like banjo players for the food chain's

higher-ups. These hors d'oeuvres
can't help me find *The Cantos*, stashed
in a box with the rest of my college books.
Siguiriya of man-sized bugs, libations

for homies who fell during the long trek
up my attic stairs. These spiders, sacrificing
whatever spiders do in a dust-blessed
space full of a language they tried to forget.

On this morning when creek and gulf
handshake sky, my attic is absent of verse
except for the ping of roof water, the caesura
of moving gifts still in their original plastic.

TOMMY JOHNSON (c. 1896-1956)

There's jake leg blues
in this box. There's carnal
scribbling: a constellation
of bug prints in a gypsy's
biography—loose-leaf, crayon
etchings and the sun shining
on my back door some day.

Tommy Johnson, forget
about air. Ignore the wind,
shimmying with seeds
and hair. But take a nail
and a seed and I'll whittle
a twelve-string that only plays
cranial propositions.

A six-string is trouble,
but the twelve is the most hoodoo'd
mess in nature—the noise
in adverbs making spiders
grow at unnatural speeds.
The pop and settle of this attic
as it ages with arthritic grace.

Orthography of dialect, jawboning
in the mix of half-notes, shoe polish
strained through bread in a glass,
and the torso of guitar topography.
Think of Prohibition-bound Tommy
Johnson, waking up in the morning,
gut splayed in abdomen:

> *Mama, mama, mama,*
> *canned heat is killing me.*

MIGRATION

My attic is smoked with light,
nonsensical like caution tape
for Cyclops. Brazos Exterminators!
William S. Burroughs! Hear what
I'm saying. I can't find *The Cantos*
anywhere in the brazen of palmetto
skulls and lost limbs, dust reconstituting
itself between wood panel and drywall.

A window air-conditioner beats, whirs:
exhalation of not-so-conditioned air
and the bugs and the bugs' former skins
don't mind one bit. And with that,
William S. Burroughs became
an exterminator:

> *And there was an apple on her head*
> *and he did shoot with a revolver and he did miss,*
> *William Telling her face first, in the Mexican*
> *mouth Texas was once a crown for.*
> *Caught fully in the dead crest of her sleeve,*
> *he did turn tail and head North, out of Mexico,*
> *out of Texas. It was a shake down.*

Mist hangs on the Rio Grande,
recoil of workers who still follow William S.
from one wild to another, scrub brush
and dust in bucketfuls waiting on the other side.

Texans speak Spanish angrily, refusing
the lilts of the language (as my landlady says,
Don-DE AYE-sta el BAIN-YO?),
moving with a vulture's reflex
through the gathering places of migrants
willing to do all the things Texans aren't.

Because they aren't. Key-holed
by the misprint of language, *limpia*
los banos more like "limping in the barrens"
than *clean the bathrooms.*

LANDSCAPED POSTCARD AS JIMI HENDRIX

I. HEDGES

Great afro, huge hands, guitarus: mountains
here and there stretched from hardwood

and devil's dust. You strung other things—
colors thumb-picked from a dragonfly's

blink. Moons cemented in the sink
of a little girl's dreams. Free-falling from planes,

grabbing air by the fistful
have done something. Or maybe it was the army

greens and that Band of Gypsys.
How else could you peel the sea

with a bell-bottom hootenanny?
Or make a jellyfish and sea star scrap,

noses wide open? Brine and sand, reverbed
stereophonically. Strings sounding

like a woman waking up. Strungs
sounding like she still wished for sleep.

2. POSTSCRIPT

Dear Manic Depression,

You have manicured the increments
of race. *Nigger* yelled full throttle

is the blindside of meat.
All that jive-dependent geography.
Mulatto shakedown: your daddy
was a black man and your mama
was white. She was the one who
sent the letter with his address
in case you have something to say.
Here's what I have to say:
Dear Cornelius, back in '70,
you weren't thinking of the inevitable
bum-rush of coffee-colored children
or the questions: "So what exactly
are you? Mexican?" Dad, being mixed
is *feeling, sweet feeling,* like Hendrix
(half-breed of a different half,
sleeping pills and freefall):
all bootlegs and misplaced letters.

HATERS

What have you done, Cornelius?
Never mind. We know what you've done:
marrying white, creating a child

of stuttered pigmentation from disco
and chalk. In this state, anyone north
of the Red River is a Yankee—ignorant

of anything pecan and already sweetened.
Cornelius, those same Yanks think
your son is Mexican. One good thing

about Texans: they know their Mexicans.
Your son will still be madhousing bigotry's
matinee, Cornelius. Living in that special

place for the multiple checker of race
boxes, an enabler of exoticism down here.
He will be the man riding the bus

in tux and tie. Some other riders will want
him gone in that gone for good
way even though they are not sure why.

WASSILY KANDINSKY'S BOXED-UP VOICE

Ear, you're the ballast for the sound-surge.
You're the harbinger of Southern-fried voices.

You're the accent resisting an accent,
the shoulder brush for the broken string

of country music. Box-cutter slipping tape,
mitts on the grope through newsprint

from Carbondale, Rochester and Indy.
Nothing from down South, like a swimmer

who has forgotten what North is. Here's
a Kandinsky print, wrapped in plastic bubbles

that didn't work. If Kandinsky wasn't
a carpetbagger, he should have been.

Ear, only someone who scoured the Texas
wild for a house with more than one story

sees the natural shock of yellow in tumbleweeds,
their blue wagon wheel innards. Pioneer red

orbited by dust: one primary hung up on another.
The winner becomes a free-hand moon.

Or free-wheeling ear. Or free-range pupil
of magenta and azure. The union of seen

and forgiven in packing material: year-old
weather forecasts, my friend the pitcher in black

and blacker on the sports page giving up another
home run, and Kandinsky's *Farbstudie*

Quadrate, almost as old as baseball, reprinted
cheaply like this until the gloved ear is gristle.

"AMERICA'S FIRST AND FOREMOST BLACK SUPERSTAR"

Gotta be a frame: Luke Cage, Hero for Hire stuck
in Texas. Me—luckier than any *seven* dudes
you know—left in a box, stashed in a jive-ass attic.
What's the beef, man? This ain't no shakedown,
but it smells like Seagate all over again: one cell
leads to another and the story don't never finish.
Who's hiring me in this box? Sure, them foxes
are here with me, but I never get at 'em unless
I'm bailing those broads out of one scrape or another.
And I still don't get no residuals. Christmas,
what's the point of being a hero for hire when you
give out more free shit than a schoolyard pusher?
I got bullet-proof skin and I'm meaner
than Jerome Mackey *and* Jim Kelly in a paper bag.
But what good is steel skin if it bounce
the same blades and boots all the time?
I'll give you five to one it ain't fun. Let Cage
get at some of that Texas barbeque. Let Cage bang
some Southern heads on the way. Christmas,
let Cage change his threads. I've been sporting
blue pants and a yellow shirt since '71. Forget
this chain-link for a belt or the metal wristbands.
Dig it, I just want to step out for a minute—
I hear those black power muthas calling stereotype.
But they don't say nothing about that voodoo mixing,
corn-rowed chump, the Witchdoctor. They don't say
nothing about my boy the Black Panther. Man,
those boys at Marvel even gave me a white sidekick:
Iron Fist. A white boy who knows kung fu, winging
a black man. Ain't that something?

COLLOQUIALISM

Being a color in Texas is to wake stressed
from being. To wake in a panhandled lethargy
of dust and heat, a mishmash of hazards
flashing a downpour.
                                    Bad to be black,
worse to be a mixed indetermination.
At the pawn shop, burrito joint, hotel lobby—
the neck hurts, swiveling toward what could be.
In Chicago, it's called a *padlock:*

1. Strap a member of a rival gang to the ride's
bumper, face up, with a chain or rope.

2. Drag him along the slow asphalt, preferably
in daylight.

3. Leave said gangster where he can be found.
If alive, concrete burns and abrasions
will message the other gangs not to mess
with the block.

In Jasper, it's called *rolling a tire.*
A kid's game catch-all: still about turf
and blocks, but they are *counties* in Texas.
Ask James Byrd, Jr. how dark
in Texas is the great unequalizer.

Ask Jesse Washington about automobile fixation
and the resonance of dirt roads and fire.
Ask either of them about the way *howdy*
barbs if said right. Behind the refrigerator magnet

Alamos and gallon-sized hats, there's a swimming
hole full of muck and snakes because this dirt
doesn't get muddy. It's miraculous.
Gravel stays sharp, tires keep their pigment,
and a slit throat stays slit, Texas rain or Texas sun.

TEXAS HOLD 'EM WITH GAUDÍ PLAYING CARDS

1. IN HAND:

Five of Spades

Knowing he would be soup,
a tortoise flippers a wish
for salt water. He is squared
by spiraled pillar concrete
and sing-song concrete
with a real hatred for civil war
and tarragon. This is what happens
when you can live half in
and half out of the drink.

Queen of Hearts

Just like a heart:
lopsided, wrong-angled,
rimmed with taffeta
like a triangle built
by somebody who flunked
geometry. Bits of mica.
Here, the heart
is an air duct. Up in here,
wires criss-cross
to keep out the 'coons.

2. COMMUNITY:

Jack of Spades

There's a clown hunkered
in a flowerpot of my head.

Demonically, like Eddie
Hazel with a comb
instead of a guitar.
This clown had a poppy flower
on each shoulder
like a colonel on the take.
He knew "demon" means
"knowledge" in Greek.

Six of Clubs

Bear-trap mouth,
steel with corrugated tongue,
you've got sheet music instead
of ears. You've got elevator up
buttons instead of eyes.
Where did you get those?
How did all that rust
become ornamental?

Two of Spades

Sea-stars hang as spire
like a jester's hat.
Who's doing the jesting now?
Not the misnamed fish
crusting in the breeze.
Not the jester or his envy
of the roof's duality.
An apartment designed
by Gaudí has a waiting
list longer than genealogy.
Who's jesting now?

NATURE'S CYCLE

Scavenger, modern flim flam
of mogul and custodian. Scavenger,
postlude to the splintering of wagon

wheels, rearranger of savannahs
and mosquitoes—there was
a buzzard in my driveway today.

It wasn't one of those goofy
cartoon birds that doesn't know
head from hoof and spends days

chasing the same thin-limbed hare.
This buzzard had its game together.
It spread its wings like a promotion,

miserable feathers bustling a dust
cloud. Its yawning beak, chipped
and uneven from cutting dead things.

But it's not that cut and dried.
The dead know their buzzards,
know this hustler was more interested

in his own build than raccoon
remains. It was a clergyman before
the offering: flapping a cloud of gravel

and twigs, daring me to come forward
and face facts. Scavenger, what
do you do, meeting something

that prefers you dead? What do
you say to the bird that will be there
in the end, two thieves or no?

GREEN JEANS

come from soil reduction,
long horns shaped from index
and pinkie extensions.

Lawn gnomes who love
nothing more than the clap
of a starter's pistol between

furrows. In Texas, cornrows
are landscaping. Or is that
a scarecrow, crouched

in crasher's position? It's like
the man says, in Texas
brothers don't ask—they just

run. Smart Estevancio sidestepped
this dirt patch like crocodile
heads in Pitfall. There is a plastic

spoon pressing down this state's
tongue that makes *dat*
from *acrobatic*. The actual

spelling is somewhere between
El Paso and the first town
in Oklahoma. Between Cormac

McCarthy and Wooderson
repping three-fingeredly
while Beck does the hot dog

dance in seersucker:
Going back to Houston
to get me some pants.

FLIGHT REFLEX

It must be winter in this part of Texas
because the grackles are posse-d up.
They toupee rooftops and wires.
They ornament trees and anything
else with room and resilience
for beak and claw. Anything
that doesn't move much.

And always, that damn epistle
of chalk and fingernail.
                              And always,
grackles signify the need for unity
in Texas, whether bird, black, or both.

It must be winter because it feels
like spring and the man-sized bugs
have split for wherever bugs go
because of the grackles.
Like urban flight, only not, and the trees
naturally crooked for hanging
hang just a little lower, their leaves
chilling in the surplus cusp of winter.

Wheels of
Steel

WHEELS OF STEEL

I got me two songs instead of eyes—
all swollen and blacked out

like the day after a lost fight. Two
jigsaws spinning, buzzing the backdrop

for woodshop or emcee, bar mitzvah
or afterset. *It's DJ Run, DMC rocking*

without a band, but not without me.
I make it rain. I make it rain on these

shined up rims still spinning after the car
stops. Dubs kind of grind like me

in their perpetuity. I'm the Wizard
of Oz if Oz was a fish fry in July.

Call me Master of the Cracked Fingers.
One song spins forward, the other

back to repeat itself: *Every day I'm*
hustlin'. Every day I'm hustlin'. Baby,

I'm the layaway payment on a Ferris
wheel. My songs orbit parking lots

and rent parties like the crazy lady's
eyes when she finds out her lover man

already left . . . *It's all because of you,*
I'm feeling sad and blue. One of my songs

spins backward, while the other plays
forward like sugar mixing in to make

the grape. My joints are the pinwheels
in this parade of moonwalks and uprocks:

See, I like to get down, Jack.

THIS ONE'S ON THE ONE

. . . the one about me.
    —Q-Tip

What lovely backyards
in the neighborhood
of crossing over: *keeping*

it real a musing, stick-pinned
to the marrow. Somebody
else's business can't be held

accountable for the skin's
synthesis, for fox fur coats,
chicken and orange juice

with starlets, or the inevitable
sunlit shaft from the record
company. Music business,

sweet disinterested landmark.
Great emulsifier, eraser
for the pencil's half-steps.

Smoother of aphasia, sun dial
for all things slang and giggly.
Schiele sunflower in the eye

of the beholder. When
was the last time someone
said *the one about me* outside

of music's raw and remixed
context without smoothing
sideburns and eyebrows into

a couture of pimp-gaminess?
Next the nose's corners, rankles
up like a holy roller passing

a bar. How easily selfish
things transcribe themselves
over rock 'em sock 'em

beats. Q-Tip, you've created
a mosh pit of throwback
jerseys and soul patches pointing

out *happy* and *has-been*
for a crowd who ain't hearing it.
Like Chinese sign language

of Joni Mitchell's voice.
Like explaining why your record
fancifully spins in the warp.

PIMP LIMP

For Flava Flav, circa 1993

On *Flavor of Love,* you crowed:
Your man Flava Flav's a pimp.
P-I-M-P! from the balcony.
A cascade of kiss and tell
on the woman walking in weaved
shame past the pool: head bowed,
bra tucked in armpit, heels clicking
maestro quick as early morning
sunbathers peeped upward
from behind sunglasses wondering
who disguised a lawn jockey
in a silk robe. It didn't have
to be this way. Fifteen years ago,
you took a jet-setting break once
a month to visit one of your girlfriends
in Bloomington. Me and my boys
hating on you before there was name
for hateration. Before a football
player's overtures finally pried
that woman loose from your clocked
embrace. The time she cut you loose,
you came to town in a limousine
on a doughnut with a dented back
door. It was sunny, and you got
out of that limping car
with a matching limp to the applause
of me and my boys laughing.
You put your Gazelles on,
kissed two jeweled peace fingers
and tossed them to the crowd.

GNOSIS

For Rik

Little brother, everything wants
to be water: afros, trombones,

Jack Purcells, tulips stretching
in the backyard. They all wish

a return to seaweed and sand,
to fish skins spit back because

they have no flavor. Everything
wants water's obstinacy.

Envy doesn't cover it. The time
you snagged my Sunday shirt,

you still couldn't play basketball.
Want's remix clicked beat by beat.

Better to try fitting into a glass
or warping wood. Or rising up,

disregarding mass. Turning the moon
on its ear time and time again, until

watches are set to you. Little
brother, we want because water

unflinches the secret moments
of our lives like thumbprints on a glass.

ALMOST INTERVENTION

My little brother lives
in Indianapolis
with its suburban rabbits

and warrens of junkies.
The neighbor's mutt
growls at what he knows

is there. Maybe corn
kernels and tassels dressed
up as humidity. Maybe

the thin-lipped vinyl
in the siding. I don't know
what it means to need

something more than you
need you. My brother
shifts from today to yesterday

in a halo of weed smoke,
slides down the concrete
driveway without mom's

permission into somebody
else's rusted minivan. He's
geometric, all points leading

to the same happenstance.
He is a porch swing
with the bolts loose.

THE MONTICELLO GRAVEYARD

It would be easier not to bury
the dead at all. No need
to round up wayward sisters,

brothers cradling hangovers
like hundred dollar shoes
on the way to the ball court

for that early morning car ride
north to the graveyard full of white
people who would run

from our familial relationship
if the dead could still
get traction. On the drive up,

I learned how math works
in our family from my brother's
phone message: *Since she*

*was only a grandma half
of the time, I'll be at the funeral
but I'm skipping the wake.*

That morning, the sun highlighted
vowels on tombstones,
leaving consonants in the awkward

position of being needed
but not seen. My brother was still
on acid when we joined

the ranks of the cousins who got
Christmas gifts from Grandma
carrying her coffin to its last

place. That morning, there
was no backyard for her to send
us to while explaining us away.

THIS BE THE VERSE

It is the 21ˢᵗ Century.
    —Radiohead

This is the skin they put me in,
my mum and dad. Remixed melanin,

olio for the asthmatic and color blind.
See how it bronzes on command.

See how my hybrided daughter looks
darker while on the beach with me.

If my skin was a chicken wing,
I'd lick my eyebrows before

code switching inflections.
If my skin were a woman, I'd check

my leopard print steering wheel
at the door. I'd transform my crust

of rust and sea salt into something
more 21ˢᵗ Century. Borges said,

Things belong to the past quite quickly,
so I'd throw some butane on my funk

transistors. Face paint my brown
band aid convocation. Toss my sweaty

"Free South Africa" muscle shirt
to the crowd at the recycling bin.

I'd leave it to the ghetto fabulous
to ID the magical backspin of skin.

SAMPLED BIOGRAPHY

For Stacey

KNOCK KNEES

In the picture, they rub together
timpanically, hodge-podge
of too-high tube socks and too-big
teeth going all directions.
Like magnolia petals if you've
never seen the flower.

ATLANTA TREES

Piney enough, sure.
Tall enough, sure,
but not so tall as to foresee

the misnomer in *Southern Belle*
or that what we can really see
of the South will have to do.

GAITHER

Your nanny is broke down in the picture,
but the stories speak of a different
woman—mean mother of a drunk,

drunk mother who means
to show you all the things
you shouldn't know, Georgia peach.

VOICE

Potentate of first-hand smoke:
gruff when riled, gruffer
when content. All the things
a voice should be, pranks and more
pranks, diction and some more
of that imposed stuff—
Pinyin of the South.

THE SOUTH

Another unfinished afternoon:
time's ribcage gummed
with cobbler and hypnosis.

WHAT I LOVE

The inertia I can't see, but was told is.
Addendum of morning's vertigo, point A
and point B and the hair it leaves.
If momentum can be rephrased, light there
is light wherever, pinioned on the gravity
of your question-mark eyes.

RAMIFICATION

Woman, I've got the blues, like an ugly
of cat-gut and malt liquor. Maybe uglier.
Woman, all the roughage in the world

won't set things straight: no jailhouse blues,
no frozen dinners clockworked on the table.
Sovereignty co-opted from your homeplace,
just you and the words I love.

MULATTO EGO REMIX

This is a hell-bent invitation
to my other ego:
that hybrided trait grunt,
that warble of sum and funk.

A swollen thing, a mixing
thing—browns and browns,
whether skin or feather.
Can I say that?

Where skin meets feather
it's last night's spill left over:
like wine on terrycloth
like anything made of pleather.
Brown skin doubled
or dubbed together.

Redundancy: hobnailed
for the hook inside the craw.
Mixed beats is all straw
like the meat inside the scarecrow.

Ego, you's a silly Jim Crow creeper.
You's the dark peeper
in the Glee Club. Ben Harper
or Vin Diesel before the name
change and the shaved head.

Syndication time, they call
it *dub*. But name-calling
is thingification, no matter what
white folks say.

No matter what black folks do,
remixing the letters in a name
like a convocation doesn't rearrange
the phonetic frown.

Because misnaming
is mismanagement: LaToya
still means "female toy."

The same way a "turkey"
wasn't heard as *tasty* turkey
until Estevancio christened
the bird "ugly peacock."

All those colors couldn't protect
it from being a meal.
All that red waddling couldn't
keep the turkey out of season.

Foul language is still foul
and ducking is called "ducking"
for a reason. What's turkeying?

LANGUAGE MIXOLOGY

Half brother of the same halves,
simulacra is fancy for "absent."

Like *banging* means "good"
or *off the chain* means "good."

The same way *off the hook* forgets
the phone, I'm forgetting the space

between Oregon and North
Carolizzay, daylight savings time

and the addition of the "-izzay."
So silly that suffix, verbed blackface

for black folks. So here you are
bouncing verbs without the face

paint like an empty room bounces
echoes: "The Mulatto Question,"

a question of remixing our name
or re-envisioning our cliché

like Bonz Malone saying, *Life
is beautiful. It's just the shit in it*

that's fucked up over vocals keys
looped like a fishhook. Didn't he know

piano is necessary in any mulatto blues?
Black key for one woman or white

key for two women. You should
be writing and that combination

is feminine. We've got a disputed
lineage, like Arizona before

Estevancio named it. We've got all
kinds of folks acting like Estevancio,

get it? Mixed man, mixed man,
states weren't called *states*, even though

the pedigreed mountains, the high-
styling lizards were already in place.

NOTES

"Seven Days of Falling": The poem's title comes from an album by the Esbjörn Svensson Trio and is dedicated to Esbjörn Svensson (1964–2008).

"Domo Arigato, Mr. Mulatto (Dub Style)": The italicized sections are remixed lyrics from Styx's "Domo Arigato, Mr. Roboto."

"Winter / Weird Fishes": The poem is inspired by Radiohead's "Weird Fishes / Arpeggi."

"Ode to Fela": *Obiri* is a house of mourning. After the death of a husband, Ibo wives are traditionally required to spend three months in the *obiri* mourning their husbands.

"The Attic": *Siguiriya* is a form of flamenco music belonging to the *cante jondo* category.

"Tommy Johnson": The end quote is from Johnson's song, "Canned Heat Blues."

"Haters": The poem is inspired by "Ain't Sayin' Nothin' New," by The Roots.

"Green Jeans": Estevancio was an African slave who accompanied Álvar Núñez Cabeza de Vaca exploring the American Southwest. He is identified as the first non-Indian to see the area now called Arizona. The end quote is from "Lord Only Knows," by Beck.

"Wheels of Steel": In order, the quoted lyrics are from Run DMC, "King of Rock"; Fat Joe, "Make It Rain"; Rick Ross,

"Hustlin'"; Doug E. Fresh and the Get Fresh Crew, "La Di Da Di"; and A Tribe Called Quest, "God Lives Through."

"This One's On the One" references Janet Jackson's "Got 'Til It's Gone." The song is yet another reason everyone should miss A Tribe Called Quest, Black Sheep, and The Pharcyde.

"This Be the Verse" is an homage to Philip Larkin's poem of the same name filtered through lyrics from Radiohead's "Bodysnatchers."

"Language Mixology": Bonz Malone's quote is from De La Soul's song "The Grind Date." The poem is dedicated to Daniel Wideman.

PENGUIN POETS

JOHN ASHBERY
Selected Poems
Self-Portrait in a Convex Mirror

TED BERRIGAN
The Sonnets

JOE BONOMO
Installations

PHILIP BOOTH
Selves

JIM CARROLL
Fear of Dreaming: The Selected Poems
Living at the Movies
Void of Course

ALISON HAWTHORNE DEMING
Genius Loci

CARL DENNIS
New and Selected Poems 1974-2004
Practical Gods
Ranking the Wishes
Unknown Friends

DIANE DI PRIMA
Loba

STUART DISCHELL
Backwards Days
Dig Safe

STEPHEN DOBYNS
Velocities: New and Selected Poems, 1966–1992

EDWARD DORN
Way More West: New and Selected Poems

AMY GERSTLER
Crown of Weeds: Poems
Ghost Girl
Medicine
Nerve Storm

EUGENE GLORIA
Drivers at the Short-Time Motel
Hoodlum Birds

DEBORA GREGER
Desert Fathers, Uranium Daughters

God
Men, Women, and Ghosts
Western Art

TERRANCE HAYES
Hip Logic
Wind in a Box

ROBERT HUNTER
Sentinel and Other Poems

MARY KARR
Viper Rum

WILLIAM KECKLER
Sanskrit of the Body

JACK KEROUAC
Book of Sketches
Book of Blues
Book of Haikus

JOANNA KLINK
Circadian

JOANNE KYGER
As Ever: Selected Poems

ANN LAUTERBACH
Hum
If In Time: Selected Poems, 1975–2000
On a Stair
Or to Begin Again

CORINNE LEE
PYX

PHILLIS LEVIN
May Day
Mercury

WILLIAM LOGAN
Macbeth in Venice
Strange Flesh
The Whispering Gallery

ADRIAN MATEJKA
Mixology

MICHAEL MCCLURE
Huge Dreams: San Francisco and Beat Poems

DAVID MELTZER
David's Copy: The Selected Poems of David Meltzer

CAROL MUSKE
An Octave above Thunder
Red Trousseau

ALICE NOTLEY
The Descent of Alette
Disobedience
In the Pines
Mysteries of Small Houses

LAWRENCE RAAB
The History of Forgetting
Visible Signs: New and Selected Poems

BARBARA RAS
One Hidden Stuff

PATTIANN ROGERS
Generations
Wayfare

WILLIAM STOBB
Nervous Systems

TRYFON TOLIDES
An Almost Pure Empty Walking

ANNE WALDMAN
Kill or Cure
Manatee/Humanity
Structure of the World Compared to a Bubble

JAMES WELCH
Riding the Earthboy 40

PHILIP WHALEN
Overtime: Selected Poems

ROBERT WRIGLEY
Earthly Meditations: New and Selected Poems
Lives of the Animals
Reign of Snakes

MARK YAKICH
The Importance of Peeling Potatoes in Ukraine
Unrelated Individuals Forming a Group Waiting to Cross

JOHN YAU
Borrowed Love Poems
Paradiso Diaspora